Pang   Tseng - Ying

20 Year Retrospective

Selected Works

Cover painting: Mystic Cave
1981
9" x 25"

FORWARD

A book on the art of Pang is long overdue. This retrospective constitutes a modest attempt to present a sample of this remarkable artist's representative works, with 50 color and 10 black and white plates, carefully chosen over a span of two productive decades.

We believe the works of Pang speak for themselves and that they will stand the test of time. Since numerous critics have eloquently lauded his talent over the past twenty years, we consider anything that we may have to add on the subject superfluous. It is our hope that, through this book, a wider audience will be able to appreciate and enjoy Pang's work.

We wish to thank the following people for their contribution in rendering this book into completion:

Ellen Klein for researching and organizing the main text.
Craig Caldwell for layout and graphic design.
Ravay Snow for copy editing and typing.
Jeff Cooper of Atelier Julian for superb photography work.
Terry Pryde of Lanman Co. for accurate four-color separation.

T.T. Nieh
Publisher

Pang Tseng-Ying's journey from the Orient to the United States spanned a distance far greater than any map can show. From the highly disciplined formality of the East to the broadly interpretive self-expression of the West, he crossed an ideological expanse of more than 4,000 years. Compared to the long tradition of oriental art, the two decades of paintings exhibited in this retrospective are like the swift flourish of an artist's bamboo-handled brush. Yet the marvelous beauty of Pang Tseng-Ying's delicate watercolors, painted during the 20 years that he has lived in the United States, bespeaks a transformation of Chinese aesthetics as remarkably subtle as the metamorphosis of a mulberry leaf into silken thread.

Pang has enriched the modern art world of the West, but, even more, he has enlivened the artistic spirit of the East that was hobbled for centuries by the inordinate homage paid to the ancient masters. His works seem to urge 20th century Chinese artists to heed the words of Matsuo Basho, the 17th century Japanese poet: *"Do not seek to follow in the footsteps of the men of old; seek what they sought."* The selected paintings in this retrospective eloquently reveal the artistic virtuosity that Pang has developed as a result of embarking upon his own quest for self-knowledge. Speaking in 1987, he said, "I think, maybe now I honestly can call myself an artist."

Born in Tokyo, Japan, in 1916, Pang grew up in Peking, China, where he began a conventional art education at a very young age. His mother, who was a medical doctor and an amateur artist, taught him the rudiments of brush calligraphy. By the time he was eight years old, he had progressed to the point that she arranged for two tutors to come to their home to teach him both calligraphy and painting.

For centuries, these two art forms were the foremost activities pursued by the more affluent Chinese. In fact, calligraphy and painting are directly related through the ink-dipped brush that imparts the free-flowing qualities so much admired in each.

"All my life," Pang says, "I've wanted to be an artist." He sold his first painting, a watercolor of a peach tree, when he was 11 years old. "All of my works," he says, "were very traditional at that time."

Pang's fluency with the paint brush was

painstakingly acquired by assidously steeping himself in the compositions and techniques of the time-honored masters. The ''Six Principles'' of painting, enumerated by Hsieh Ho in the sixth century A.D. and adhered to by every succeeding generation of artists, were his guide:

The first is, that through a vitalizing spirit, a painting should possess the movement of life.

The second is, that by means of the brush, the structural basis should be established.

The third is, that the representation should so conform with the objects as to give their likenesses.

The fourth is, that the coloring should be applied according to their characteristics.

The fifth is, that through organization, place and position should be determined.

The sixth is, that by copying, the ancient models should be perpetuated.

(From **The Spirit of the Brush,** translated by Shio Sakanishi, (**Wisdom of the East Series,** 1957).)

When he was 18 years old, Pang entered the Chunghua College of Art in Peking. ''It was here,'' he says, ''that I began to learn about Western painting. But even when I changed from the Oriental to the Western way of painting, I could not entirely get away from the old, very traditional style.''

Ironically, this was because the European artists whose works he studied had themselves been influenced by the Oriental style. Since at least the second half of the 19th century, when Japanese prints and designs increasingly found their way into the West, these artists had been exposed to the aesthetics of the Far East. Enamored with the brilliant mineral colors and abstract designs that the Japanese had added to the bold Chinese brush strokes, with which Pang was familiar, the European painters had experimented with composition and technique in ways that evoked in him a feeling of déjà vu.

In the Fauvist style of Henri Matisse, whose colorful paintings looked as flat as wallpaper, and in the Abstract Expressionism of Franz Kline, noted for his dynamic, black and white "Action Painting," Pang saw the West's modern equivalents of the traditional Eastern styles of painting and calligraphy. It was in the work of the French Impressionists, however, that he most readily identified the Orient's oblique contribution to the art of the West.

"For me," Pang says, "Cezanne, Van Gogh, and Gaugin were most inspirational." In Gaugin's **Self-Portrait,** for example, he recognized the Japanese influence behind the artist's bright swatches of color and firm, heavy lines. He also saw how Degas, intrigued by the manner in which the Japanese used vertical space, was moved to paint **The Dancer** dramatically foreshortened, as if he were viewing her from above.

When Pang completed his studies at the Chunghua College of Art, he chose to further his education not in Europe but in Japan. He received a scholarship to the Nippon University in Tokyo, where he earned his Master's degree in Art.

It was while he was a student in Japan that Pang's style of painting totally changed. "While I was studying painting," he says, "I took a class in philosophy. That one philosophy teacher did more to deepen my insight into artistic expression than did any other teacher I met."

In China, Pang had been taught to think of creativity as something that came to artists only after they had achieved proficiency in the composition and color of the great master painters. Under the tutelage of his philosophy professor, Pang discovered that creative values could be educed by the artist himself. "This part of my education," he says, "was extremely important for me. My whole way of thinking about the traditional aesthetic values changed."

Pang says that his years in Japan opened up for him "an entirely new world…Until I was about 25 years old, I had painted only still life; the traditional way of learning Chinese art. In Japan, though, art teachers had gotten away from this method. Instead, they taught by having us paint from real life."

For instance, he says, "They would tell the

students, 'Go one or two miles away, close to the train station, where you can see the railroad tracks. Find a tree by the side of the tracks, the train station, and the people waiting for the train to come.' All the students would go out to the train station, and each would find different subjects for their compositions. Every student's painting would be **different**--something that never would have happened in China!''

After having spent most of his life up to that point aspiring to conform to the manner of the ancient Chinese painters, Pang found his mind and hands freed from that rigid aesthetic mold. The only limits that bound him now were those of his own creative ability.

''To be an amateur painter, like my mother was,'' he says, ''is relatively easy, when you only paint what you can put in front of you. But to paint something that emerges from inside of you--to show other people this completely original way of looking at the world--that is very difficult to do.''

So, Pang set about the arduous work of finding, in himself, the source of his own artistic reality. He developed a truly personal style and, when he was invited to enter

15" x 15¾"   1941   Dance of Twilight

one of his paintings in an exhibition of the Dokuritsu Group in Tokyo, was rewarded with the honor of second prize.

After receiving his Master's degree, Pang returned to China, where he taught art and painted for the next 25 years. While an instructor at the Chunghua College of Art, he also was appointed head of the art department of Husein Normal College in Sian. Later, he taught painting in Shenyang and Chinchow, Manchuria.

Following the communist revolution in Mainland China, Pang taught painting at the National Arts College and the Fushing School of Arts and Crafts in Taiwan. "I really liked being a teacher," he says, "because I felt I had something to offer to future artists. It's important to me to help teach the artistic tradition, but you can respect tradition without copying it. The Chinese artists are **too** traditional, and I think, therefore, it's even more important for them to learn that the beauty in a work of art comes from the inside of the artist."

20¼" x 14¾"   1950   Study of My Wife

In 1954, the National Association of Women Artists sponsored Pang's first New York one-man show, at the Argent Gallery. His works, done in oil on paper, had been exhibited previously in Mainland China, Taiwan, and Japan. **Art Digest** reported thus on the show:

> Their tenor is generally solemn and moody, especially in the landscapes, where broad and heavy rhythms and dramatic dark colors evoke expressionist overtones... There are occasional surprises, for at times Pang's palette moves from somber browns and dull greens to an almost fauve brightness, and his simple, weighty form can change, for example, to an animated dance of fiery trees against the blue night sky.

A review in **The New York Times** commented that Pang ''seized upon some aspect of a scene with genuine visionary power.'' He was similarly applauded by the **Herald Tribune:**

He has several trends of style, showing free brush work in some, flickering color or an almost Van Gogh-like turn in others and a formal somewhat abstract style in still other canvases. In all of them, he is a competent technician, direct in painting and tasteful in color...His work is influenced clearly by Western ideas.

In the early 1960's, Pang gave up oil painting and returned to watercolor. ''When I was painting in oil,'' he says, ''I was a Chinese artist painting in a Western medium. It was alien to me, and I didn't think I'd be able to paint in oil better than a Westerner could. I decided to use the medium that was more suited to who I am and what I could do. Watercolors are what I do best.''

Pang was not quite 50 years old when the then President of the Republic of China, Chiang -Kai- Shek, awarded him the President's award, the highest prize that any Chinese artist had ever received.

In 1966, with a grant from the Asia Foundation, Pang and his family emigrated to the United States. The

How Goes the Night?
1966
34" x 15"

last thing he expected to do was to take the American art
world by storm. However, when his cousin entered one of
his paintings in a contest, it won Pang his first prize in the
U.S. Within the next couple of years, he collected some two-
hundred more.

Major exhibitions then followed. In 1966 and 1967
alone, Pang exhibited in the annual shows of both the
American Watercolor Society and the Allied Artists of
America; his paintings could be seen on display at the
Brooklyn Museum, New Jersey State Museum in Trenton,
and the Berkshire Museum in Massachusetts, and he had
five one-man shows in galleries around New York City and
Detroit and a one-man show at the Hudson River Museum
in Yonkers, New York.

Since then, he has had more than 50 one-man
shows at major galleries throughout the United States,
Switzerland, and Venezuela. Aside from art galleries, his
paintings have also been exhibited at places as diverse as
the International Monetary Fund, in Washington, D.C. and
I.B.M., in Princeton, New Jersey, as well as various
museums and universities throughout the country.

In 1978, Pang was contracted by T.T. Nieh

Publishing to do a series of stone lithographs at Atelier Eleanor Ettinger in New York. After completing four sets of lithographs, the artist and the publisher decided to continue his graphic publication in another medium, namely the serigraph, in view of the inherent complexity of Pang's work in terms of the number of colors he uses and their associated brilliancy.

Since 1980, Atelier Julian of Rochester, New York, has been rendering Pang's serigraphs for exclusive distribution by T.T. Nieh Publishing. After much experimentation and technical development, the Pang serigraphs have now attained a state of perfection that are the proud possession of many collectors.

In 1983, Pang was invited back to Taiwan by the National Historical Museum of China for a retrospective show of selected works he had painted in the United States. This honor had been extended previously only to one other person, namely the great French-Chinese artist, Chao-Wu-Chi, in the mid 1970's.

Following the Taiwan exhibition, the New England Center for Contemporary Art, in Connecticut, immediately invited Pang for a similar retrospective. Center Director

Pang, his wife, and their young daughter, 1955.

Henry Riseman described Pang as ''a painter both of our time and of an era past. His pictorial language is highly disciplined, evocative of China's master painters.''

Florence Berkman, the well-known art critic, writing for **The Middleton Press** (Conn.), observed that ''Pang's paintings prove wrong Rudyard Kipling's conviction that 'East is East and West is West and ne'er the twain shall meet.'' The retrospective of Pang's watercolors, she said, ''brings together the basic techniques of Chinese art, its poetic interpretations of nature and the freedom of 20th century abstract expressionism,'' Berkman also wrote:

> These are ingratiating works on view. They invite the imagination to wander and there is a tranquility, a oneness with nature that provides the viewer with a peace that has been absent in American art indeed since the advent of abstract-expressionism.

Her remarks echoed those written several years earlier by Gordon Brown, senior editor of **ARTS Magazine:**

> He has so ably subordinated western influences to eastern moods that one can only regard his present manner as oriental. Eastern elements in Pang's inspired paintings include the free composition, the reliance on tone rather than color to establish the basic forms and the use of blank spaces as essential parts of the design. His pictures vary in their degree of reliance on western concepts...His mood is predominantly poetic and leads to philosophic meditation. He has a greater variety of brushstrokes at his command than the average western artist...With remarkable economy of means, Pang's magic brush expresses grace, strength, elegance, abruptness and freshness as the occasion may require. These are qualities that all nations can admire and understand. Pang has made a splendid contribution toward the internationalization of art while retaining rich values that are national and personal.

Writing more than one and a half centuries ago, Ku K'ai-Chih defined Chinese painting as *"Great thoughts, deftly captured."* As subsequent generations of artists sought to reproduce the images that scholars had deemed to be the highest achievements of Chinese painters, originality became less and less appreciated. It was the image, rather than the imagination, that became the essence of Chinese aesthetics.

"I painted very good paintings," Pang says, "and people liked them. But I think that my paintings did not reflect my own ideas at first, because the Chinese art education is so very traditional in its respect for the past masters. I'd have to say that, until I was about 45 years old, I was still a student. It took me that long before I learned to paint my own thoughts.''

The reward for this long period of introspection, he says, is not to be measured by the numerous awards that his paintings have earned him. Rather, the creative act is its own reward. ''Just like the scientist searches for the true laws of nature,'' Pang says, ''the artist hopes to find truth within his own awareness of the world around him. This truth, which artists seek, is what I call beauty. And every painting that results from an artist's discovery of something new is truly beautiful.''

No longer held in the thrall of the great Chinese masters, Pang has adapted their expressive brush strokes, the elegance and leanness of their style, and their powerful, graceful imagery to suit his own needs. Every day, for many hours, he works in his studio, painting deliberately, with an absorption in his work that is almost palpable.

He has an idea already in mind when he begins a painting. The idea dictates both the composition and the creation of the painting so that the idea and the movement of his hand work together, as if they were one. Holding the brush vertically, with his palm open and relaxed, his fingers firm but not rigid, he communes with the painting in a language of flowing, rhythmical strokes and subtle variations of color.

The Chinese brush has been the single most important factor in the history of Chinese painting. The brushes that Pang uses in the United States are identical to those he used in China. Mounted in simple bamboo holders, their tips are made either from the white hairs of goats and sheep or from the dark hairs of wolves. The hairs are carefully graded, both as to length and as to resilience, so that when the brush is moistened, the hairs will come to a perfect point.

Pang uses 19 kinds of Chinese rice paper and five different American-made papers in his work, selecting any given one according to the particular demands of his painting. To prepare the paper for a painting, he dips it into a pan of water, wetting both sides thoroughly. If it is an American-made paper, he crushes it in both his hands before spreading it open on a table. He does this because,

Pang at work at his New York studio, 1967.

although Chinese rice paper takes his delicate, cobwebby designs very well, American paper must be persuaded to take ink in a similar manner. In this regard, sometimes Pang also treats the paper with an alcohol wash.

With a short-handled brush, about five inches wide, and with soft, white bristles not more than one inch long, Pang brushes warm water over the entire surface of the paper; first from side to side, then top to bottom, until the paper is quite wet and lies perfectly flat on the table. If it is a paper that he has crumpled, the network of fine lines that he created will be faintly visible.

Pang then dips a brush into water and, taking up some pigment, begins to lay down areas of color. In addition to black and white, Pang's palette contains ten colors: cadmium yellow pale, lemon yellow, flame red, carmine, cadmium orange, raw umber, sky blue, Prussian blue, viridian, and permanent green deep. Nearly all of the pigments are minerals in powder form.

Great care is required to get pigments fine enough for painting on soft paper, and sometimes it is necessary to grind them again before use. This is done by grinding a small amount of pigment in a mortar, pouring in a very little amount of water, and separating out the finest powder, which floats to the surface, by pouring the colored liquid through a piece of fine silk.

Chinese ink is made of pine soot, refined and solidified with glue into sticks or blocks. When the ink is ground into powder and mixed with water, its shade may range from palest grey to deepest black.

The absorbency of the rice paper prevents Pang from making any corrections to his work; most of the time, his intense mental concentration and decisive execution abjure the possibility of second thoughts. "There are times, however," he says, "when it's as if the brush is moving on its own. I don't like that, because anyone can paint that way. The most important thing for me, I believe, is that my paintings be an expression of my conscious--not my subconscious--mind."

For Pang, a painting is the individual artist's representation of **Yu chou,** the Chinese view of the universe. Both a part of the world in which the painter lives and also a part of the artist himself, the painting exists in a space-time continuum, offering a profound statement about the nature of life.

"A work of art," Pang says, "really is three things. First, it is the past--memory. Second, it is the future--imagination. Third, it is the present--vitality. Creativity is, in essence, the story of life, and it unfolds just as surely as the future follows the past. I don't want to paint imaginary things that appear only in fantasies--I want to paint real life."

Although many of Pang's themes are derived from the real world, his paintings are not literal representations of nature. "I am a realistic painter," he says, "but what I paint, whether it's a house, or a flower, or a mountain, is entirely different from another painter's house, flower, or mountain. What I paint isn't going to look like a photograph, either--it comes from my memories and experiences, from what I feel in my heart. What's inside of me influences what I see, so when you look at my paintings, you see into me too."

In his demand for deeper meaning in his art work, Pang discards as many as one-third of his paintings. "Some artists," he says, "are satisfied with having placed colors together in an attractive way. For me, I have to find something inside of me that responds to what I see and communciates a sense of completeness."

Each painting will go through at least two mountings before it is considered finished. Ordinarily, a Chinese artist will send his watercolor painting to a specialist in **Piao-hwa,** the mounting technique. Pang accomplishes this delicate, precise, and time-consuming stage of his work by himself.

The first mounting takes place after Pang has been painting for between two and four hours. He leaves the watercolor to dry. When it is absolutely dry, he turns it face down and moistens the back thoroughly with a wide, soft brush dipped in water. He removes the excess water from the paper by blotting it with tissues. If the paper is not wet enough, it will pucker; if too wet, it will stretch. The amount of water necessary to make it completely smooth and flat depends upon the weight of the paper.

Pang then applies wallpaper paste to the back of the painting in quick, thick strokes, to avoid over-wetting the paper. When the back of the painting is completely covered with paste, he lays a dry precut sheet of backing paper over it.

The backing paper has been cut to allow a one-inch margin extending beyond the painting on all sides. With a thinner paste, he covers the one-inch border, then carefully places the joined sheets against a smooth, upright, wooden board.

Brushing over the surface with a dry, soft, wide brush, to ensure that the pasted border is firmly affixed to the mounting board, Pang has completed the process. It will be at least one and a half days before the paste is dry enough for it to continue working on the painting.

''My paintings,'' Pang says, ''represent my personal and cultural values. They are drawn from my experiences and education. I am going back to my roots--the Oriental

Pang at work, assisted by his wife, 1987.

approach to nature and to the world. My paintings originate in the Oriental concepts, but it's my experiences that make my paintings different from anyone else's''.

Predominantly a landscapist, Pang's misty slopes and tiny human figures combine the aesthetics of the Chinese masters with his own personal artistic vision. For centuries, Chinese artists have painted landscapes with the intent that viewers should imaginatively enter into the painting and experience the mystical spirit of the scene. Human figures never assumed proportions that would suggest that man is more important than Nature's other creations.

For Pang, these little human figures have additional meaning. When asked by Florence Berkman to explain what the figures in his landscapes mean, he said that they represented the time in his life when Japan had invaded China in World War II. He and his family had to leave their home and wander in the mountains begging:

> Pang said that he could not get that period with its travails out of his mind. For a number of years he painted scenes that recalled the days of wandering for his family and for so many Chinese. Often the people from whom they begged received them with kindness; other times there was only cruelty.
> (**The Middletown Press,** Conn., Sept. 21, 1984)

Just as Pang has combined the aesthetics of the master painters with his own vivid experiences, he has also found parallels to his own inner thoughts in works by the classical Chinese poets. For example, one painting takes its name, **How Goes the Night** (1966) from the title of a poem from the **Shi King,** or Book of Odes, compiled circa 500 B.C.:

> How goes the night?
> Midnight has still to come.
> Down in the court the torch is blazing bright;
> I hear far off the throbbing of the drum.
> How goes the night?
> The night is not yet gone.
> I hear the trumpets blowing on the height;
> The torch is paling in the coming dawn.
> How goes the night?
> The night is past and done.
> The torch is smoking in the morning light;
> The dragon banner floating in the sun.
> (Translated by Helen Waddell, Mark Van Doren, ed., **An Anthology of World Poetry, 1934.)**

Of Signs and Ciphers
1966
36" x 24"

Similarly, **Of Signs and Ciphers** (1966), is taken from a phrase that appears in the eleventh century poem, **The Cicada,** by Ou-yang Hsiu:

> ...Alas, philosophy has taught
> That the transcending mind in its strange, level world
> Sees not kinds, contraries, classes or degrees.
> And if of living things
> Man once seemed best, what has he but a knack
> Of facile speech, what but a plausible scheme
> Of signs and ciphers that perpetuate
> His thoughts and phrases? And on these expends
> His brooding wits, consumes his vital breath;
> One droning out the extremity of his woe,
> Another to the wide world publishing
> His nobleness of heart!
>   Thus, though he shares
> The brief span of all creatures, yet his song
> A hundred ages echoes after him...

(Translated by Arthur Waley, Mark Van Doren, ed., **An Anthology of World Poetry,** 1934.)

Pang clearly has bridged the gap between the ancient aesthetics of the East and the 20th-century aesthetics of the West. No longer in a position where he can directly influence art students or educators in China, he has written a Chinese-language text, titled **Basic Discussions on Art.** ''I want to help the Chinese learn,'' he says, ''not to break away from tradition, but how to build upon it.''

Although he is over 70 years old, Pang continues to paint prodigiously. In addition, he gets up every day at 2 or 3 o'clock in the morning and writes. ''I can't put everything I want to say into my paintings, and it isn't possible for me to teach by demonstrating the techniques that are right for me. Every artist is different. A teacher's job is to help the student find himself, to find what the masters, themselves, sought.''

Twenty years ago, art critics predicted that ''for many collectors, Pang-watching is bound to become a fascinating pursuit.''That prediction has come true. Today, Pang's award-winning watercolors are treasured by numerous collectors throughout the world.

"When I've just finished a painting," Pang says, "I feel very happy. But I also have the feeling that the painting really isn't finished. It's not that the technique isn't complete. It's as though I know that the work of art isn't finished yet--because life itself isn't finished."

After living in the New York/New Jersey area for nearly twenty years, Pang moved to Maryland in 1985, where he now resides and maintains his studio.

Pang relaxes with his wife, 1987.

One-Man Shows (Partial Listing)

1954   First one-man show in the United States--an exhibit of oils on paper.
The Argent Gallery, New York, New York.
Sponsored by the National Association of Women Artists.

1966   **Swain Gallery,** White Plains, New York

1967   **The Hudson River Museum,** Yonkers, New York
United Nations, New York, New York
Field Gallery, Detroit, Michigan

1968   **Fairleigh Dickinson University,** Teaneck, New Jersey
Theatre Six Gallery, Metuchen, New Jersey

1969   **Artist Showcase,** Virginia Beach, Virginia
Carpet Drama Gallery, Far Hills, New Jersey
Swain Gallery, White Plains, New York
Rehoboth Art League, Rehoboth Beach, Delaware
Gallery 12, Livingston, New Jersey
Dragon Gallery, Hooksett, New Hampshire
Doo Gallery, Hargord, Connecticut

> The Hartley Gallery
> cordially invites you to attend
> a champagne reception to meet
> the internationally acclaimed artist
>
> ## TSENG-YING PANG
>
> and to preview his new water colors
> on Thursday, February 10th
> from 5 to 9 p.m.
> 234 Park Avenue North, Winter Park, Florida

1970   **Newark Gallery,** Newark, Delaware
North Carolina A and T State University, Greensboro, North Carolina

1971   **Holyoke Natural and History Mueum,** Holyoke, Massachusetts
Ruth Green's Art Gallery, Raleigh, North Carolina
Washington County Museum of Fine Arts, Hagerstown, Maryland
Columbus Museum of Art, Columbus, Georgia
Bank Haley Gallery, Southwest Georgia Art Association,
Albany, Georgia
Kunst Gallery Haudensenschild and Laubscher, Bern, Switzerland
Art Gallery of South Orange and Maplewood, New Jersey
Rome Art and Community Center, Rome, New York
Westtown School, Westtown, Pennsylvania

1972   **Fairleigh Dickinson University,** Madison, New Jersey
Galeria Bellas Arts, Caracas, Venezuela
Art 3 Association of Livingston, Inc., New Jersey

22

1973	**Ruth Green's Art Gallery,** Raleigh, North Carolina **I.B.M.,** Princeton, New Jersey
1974	**Taylor Gallery,** Provincetown, Massachusetts
1976	**St. John's University Gallery,** Jamaica, New York
1977	**International Art Expo,** Washington, D.C.
1978	**Guild Gallery,** New York, New York
1979	**Guild Gallery,** New York, New York **Venable Neslage Gallery,** Washington, D.C. **Potomac Gallery of Old Town,** Alexandria, Virginia
1980	**Steven Rosendahl Gallery,** Naples, Florida **Guild Gallery,** New York, New York **Broward Gallery,** Pompano Beach, Florida
1981	**International Art Expo,** Washington, D.C. **Rodger La Pelle Gallery,** Philadelphia, Pennsylvania **Artistic Eye Gallery,** Tuston, California **Gallerie Julian,** Alexandria, Virginia
1982	**International Art Expo,** San Francisco, California **International Art Expo,** New York, New York **Hartley Gallery,** Winter Park, Florida **Gallerie Julian,** Alexandria, Virginia
1983	**Hartley Gallery,** Winter Park, Florida **National Museum of History,** Taipei, Taiwan
1984	**New England Center for Contemporary Art,** Brooklyn, Connecticut **Gallerie Julian,** Alexandria, Virginia
1985	**Rodger La Pelle Gallery,** Philadelphia, Pennsylvania **Bond Street Gallery,** Pittsburgh, Pennsylvania
1986	**Peri-Kenneth Gallery,** South Hampton, New York

(PANG)

at

Gallerie Julian
506 KING ST. ALEXANDRIA, VA. 22314
(703) 548-6203
October 1982

Group Exhibitions (partial listing)

Allied Artists of America--New York, annual exhibitions, 1968, 1969, 1970
American Watercolor Society Annual--New York, 1966, 1967
Audubon Artists--annuals 1972, 1973, 1974
Adriance Museum, Poughkeepsie, New York, 1967, 1968
Art Classic on the Plaza--West Orange, New Jersey, 1970
Berkshire Museum--Massachusetts
Jersey City Museum--Jersey City, New Jersey
Montclair Museum--Montclair, New Jersey
Newark Museum--Newark, New Jersey
New England Annual Exhibition--Connecticut
International Art Expo--New York, New York, 1979, 1980, 1981, 1983, 1984, 1985, 1986
International Art Expo--Washington, D.C., 1979, 1980
New Jersey State Museum--Trenton, New Jersey
Westchester Art Society Annual Juried Exhibition--White Plains, New York
Brooklyn Museum--Brooklyn, New York
Painters' and Sculptors' Society of New Jersey--New Jersey
International Monetary Fund--Washington, D.C., 1970
Brockton Arts Center--Brockton, Massachusetts, 1970

Permanent Collections (partial listing)

Desert Museum-- Palm Springs, California
Indiana Museum--Indiana
New England Center for Contemporary Art--Connecticut
Town of West Orange--West Orange, New Jersey
County College of Morris-- Dover, New Jersey
National Historical Museum of China--Taipei, Taiwan
National Art Center--Taipei, Taiwan
Free Library of Philadelphia--Philadelphia, Pennsylvania
Berkshire Museum--Massachusetts
Newark Museum--Newark, New Jersey
New Jersey State Museum--Trenton, New Jersey
Brooklyn Museum--Brooklyn, New York
Brigham Young University--Provo, Utah
Utah State University--Logan, Utah

Dusk
1966
24" x 18"

Rhythm
1966
20" x 28"

Blue Stream
1966
25" x 23½"

Autumn Sonata
1966
20" x 32½"

Return of the Winter
1967
20" x 28"

Branches
1967
22½" x 17¾"

Hanging Fruit
1967
24″ x 14¾″

Moonlight
1968
35⅝" x 24½"

Red Melody
1969
18¼" x 23⅞"

Twilight Hills
1970
30" x 21"

Family Reunion
1971
34″ x 10″

Four Seasons
1973
27" x 31"

Hidden Valley
1974
25¾" x 19"

Blue Canyon
1974
16¾″ x 12½″

Flowing Spring
1976
16¾" x 22½"

Florals in Bloom
1976
23¾″ x 23¾″

Majesty
1977
24" x 20"

Floral Landscape
1977
24" x 19¼"

Village Walk
1977
11¾″ x 23½″

Goldfish Ballet
1978
24" x 31"

Swinging Fish
1978
31″ x 24¼″

The Lily Pond
1978
19⅜" x 24"

Yellow Floral
1979
16″ x 12¾″

Red Floral
1979
16" x 12"

Flower Forms
1979
18" x 18"

Autumn Breeze
1979
35½" x 23"

In the Current
1979
18½" x 37"

Pang's Twins
1980
23" x 18" each

Fantasy
1980
29" x 20"

Abstract I
1980
35½" x 23"

Untitled
1980
35⅜" x 23"

Homage to Miro I
1981
35½″ x 23″

Homage to Miro II
1981
35½" x 23"

Enchanted Village
1981
20" x 36"

Amber
1981
37" x 9"

First of spring
1982
18½" x 36"

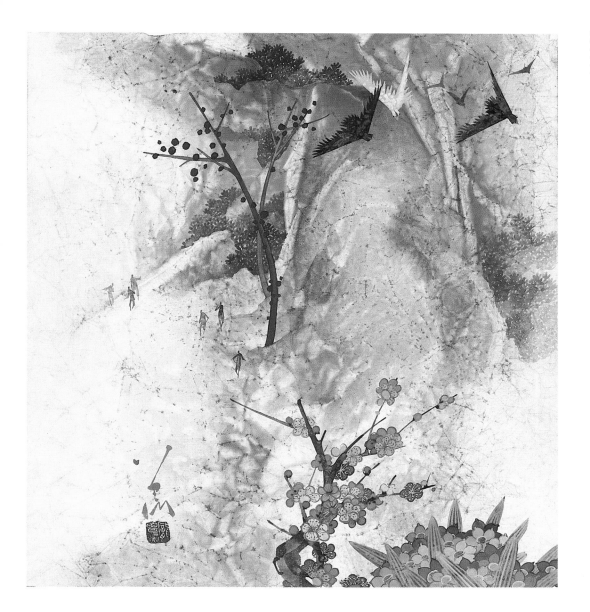

Floral Reverie
1982
18½" x17¼"

Fantastic Grouping
1982
23" x 35"

Pang's Wave
1982
37" x 10"

Ascending
1983
23⅝" x 13⅛"

Golden Pond
1984
35⅝″ x 23⅜″

Messengers
1984
40¼" x 15"

Spring Valley
1985
24¼" x 18"

Whispering
1986
16½″ x 22½″

Spring Dip
1986
18½" x 31"

Reflections
1986
16½" x 19½"

Cool Depths
1986
18″ x 31½″

Morning Mist
1986
20" x 14"